P9-BJA-958

FRONTIER NOTES

by Gordon Reid

We are proud that our son Don Reid was a part of Camrose Lutheran College. Gordon

Dedicated to Edna, who back in early 1963 while we were living in Edmonton, said "Lets start packing tomorrow," and with that we moved to High Level . . . and found home.

The contribution of the people of Alberta, through Alberta Culture, is gratefully acknowledged.

Standard Book No. 0-919213-17-0

Published by
Lower Peace Publishing Co. Ltd.
Box 509,
High Level, Alberta

FIRST PRINTING MAY, 1976
SECOND PRINTING NOV., 1976
THIRD PRINTING SEPT., 1978
FOURTH PRINTING MARCH, 1981
Printed by D. W. Friesen & Sons Ltd.
Calgary, Alberta
Head Office: Altona, Manitoba

FOREWORD

When does history of an area begin and when does it end? How is there a difference between an old-timer and a long-timer? To some in our area two years is a long time; to some in our area who were born here, old time and long time mean nothing.

History may be going back to the start of Fort Vermilion over 175 years ago or beyond, or it may be living in High Level before there is pavement.

Whatever, history is fascinating.

Thanks to folks for their pictures and time.

Gordon.

ABOUT THE AUTHOR

Gordon Reid was born in Drumheller, Alberta and raised at Delia, northeast of Drumheller.

In 1951, he married Edna Pottage of Sedgewick, Alberta and together they gained a love of the north while living at Slave Lake, Alberta from 1954 to 1959. They moved to High Level in 1963.

Gordon is a successful businessman in High Level and is active in the community.

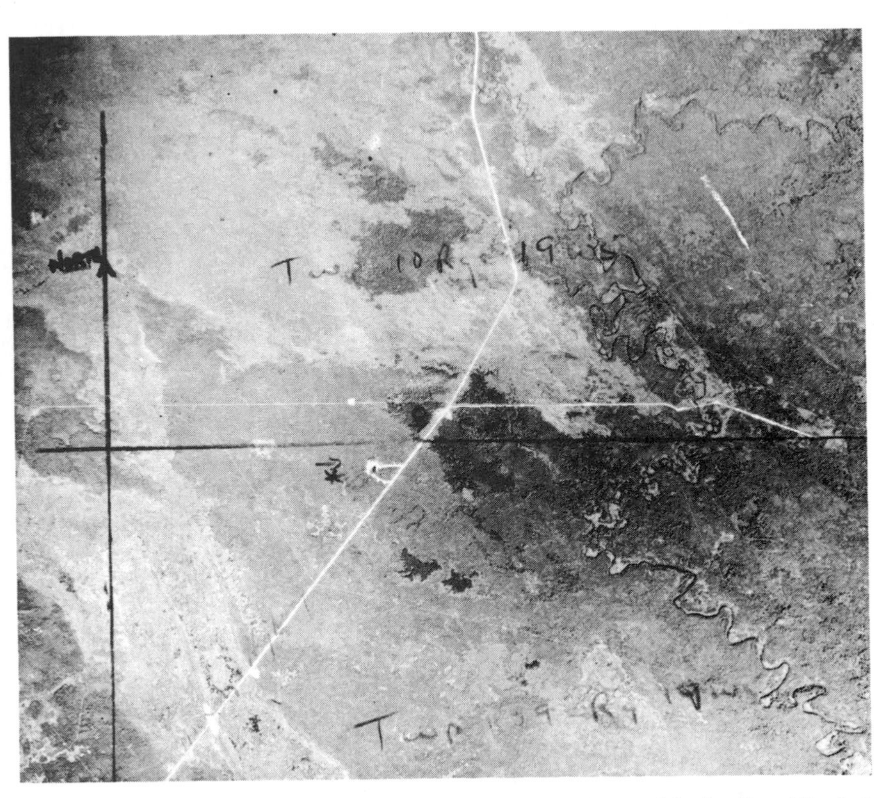

High Level from the air in 1948 showing the Mackenzie Highway and the junction of the Fort Vermilion Trail. Imperial Oil is drilling a well at the sight of the present school. Alberta Government Photo.

FRONTIER NOTES

THE RAILROAD ARRIVES — A Town is Assured

Travelling north on the dusty Mackenzie Highway during the summer of 1963, you could not help but get a thrill when you could see the work trains on the Great Slave Lake Railway which nearly parallels the highway.

There was great speculation in that part of Northern Alberta - if the railway arrived a community was a certainty.

Naturally the 75 or so residents in High Level were apprehensive. The arrival or the failure to arrive of the ribbon of steel meant as much then as it did in the pioneer railway days of the Southern prairies.

Slowly, but surely, the steel moved northward all summer un-

First train to arrive in High Level, November, 1963. Taken by Ernie Duchesne.

til near the end of October the steel crossed the Mackenzie Highway about 5 miles south of town. Everyone began to speculate on the date and time of arrival of that precious first train.

It was Saturday night November 2nd, and a crowd, as usual, had gathered for the weekend shopping at the wee general store facing the Mackenzie Highway and the railway right-of-way. In the store were pioneer farmers who had hauled their grain 180 miles south by road to Grimshaw for years. There were also young businessmen and their wives who had speculated their livelihood on the arrival of the train. There were young people hoping that they could find a new future in the North. Perhaps there were 25 in that store when long time farmer John Gibb opened the door to leave and just as the door opened that beautiful train blasted, forever it seemed, its shrill whistle. Its outline could be seen moving into position near the highway crossing of the Fort Vermilion junction.

The walls of that small store rocked as the crowd cheered and farmers openly cried for joy. Someone bought pop all around and everyone moved onto the small platform sidewalk outside the store in a grand salute.

Truly we had "arrived" and there was no turning back on progress now.

We who have lived through this recent bit of Heritage Alberta can feel the happiness of pioneer days in the west some 50 to 60 years earlier, when they looked with apprehension on the arrival of the first steam railway train.

July, 1963. Left: Esso Garage and Cafe. Centre: Reid's Store. Right: Former store about to be converted to High Level's first police barracks. Canadian Coachways "Bruck" in front with Howard MacKay's water truck.

CONSIDERATION

Bill and Lil Willows lived in High Level a few years ago and Lil gave us this little poem when she left High Level.

Pray don't find fault with the man who limps
Or stumbles along the road,
Unless you have worn the shoes he wears
Or stumbled beneath his load.

He may have tacks in his shoes that hurt
Though hidden away from view,
Or the burden he bears, placed on your shoulders
May cause you to falter too.

Don't sneer at the man who is down today
Unless you have felt the blows,
That caused his fall, or felt the same
That only the fallen knows.

You may be strong but still, the blows
That were his, if dealt to you
In the self same way, at the self same time
May cause you to stumble too.

Don't pelt him with words or stones
Unless you are sure, yea doubly sure,
That you have no sins of your own
For you know perhaps if the tempter's voice
Should whisper as soft to you
As it did to him when he went astray
It could cause you to falter too.

A FATHER'S LOVE

Four young fellows from High Level headed for Fort Vermilion one evening in the late fall of 1963 for an hour or two of fun.

As they started down the river hill towards the ferry, terror gripped them for they realized the brakes on their car were failing. There was no time to bail out. There were no other vehicles on the ferry.

With terrific force they hit the ferry decking and through the 2 inch safety cable on the river side they tore, nose-diving into the water with all four still in the car.

Immediately an alert was dispatched to the R.C.M.P. at Fort Vermilion and almost immediately three of the young fellows surfaced and were rescued by the ferryman.

Young, good-looking Larry Freeman didn't make it. It was presumed that he was trapped in the car.

Recovery operations and dragging operations continued until

late the next day. The car was hooked and surfaced - empty of the body of Larry.

The family and friends as well as the R.C.M.P. continued dragging operations as long as the late fall days would allow.

After a few days the search was discontinued by all except for his persistent father, John, who fought chunks of ice drifting down the river. He bought the largest fish hooks in all the little stores in the area.

By a miracle on the last evening before the river froze over, he hooked the collar of the body of his beloved son and surfaced him.

The ordeal had aged poor John and his wife Jean by years, but the relief on their faces was great.

At the mill the next day they purchased the finest lumber for a coffin. The general store had five yards of black satin material in stock and some coffin handles were located in Steen River, 110 miles north. They arrived on the bus.

The father bought the best underwear in stock in the store and was so happy that his son could be dressed in warm clothing.

The funeral was held in Paddle Prairie for there was no graveyard in High Level. Crowds came from far and wide to pay homage not only to a fine, young fellow but to a brave and devoted father.

GEORGE PORTER — AN ELK

An interesting feature of the organization and institution of High Level B.P.O. Elks Lodge No. 508 on June 27th, 1966 was the installation of what was possibly the first full-blooded Eskimo into the Elks Lodge in Canada. Installed as a charter member was George Porter.

As Canadians, we were proud to have George and his wife Effie living in High Level. George was station agent on the relatively new Great Slave Lake Railroad. They were here from Gjoa Haven on King William Island in the North West Territories about 900 air-miles north of High Level.

"RESTURANT"

A report from now retired, Mrs. Arma Robinson says that money was scarce after she and Pete took out a homestead eight miles east and one mile south of High Level in 1957.

Arma took over the restaurant in High Level in 1958 and ran it for two years, catering to truckers, fishermen, trappers as well as farmers from LaCrete, Fort Vermilion, and Rocky Lane on their way to Grimshaw with their grain and to do their shopping there.

Arma commented, "The cafe was simple, maybe even crude but business was good. Full course meals were $1.00 per plate. In winter, ice had to be melted for water but ever present was the

Keleman's High Level Motel and Restaurant with new store behind. October, 1955.

fancy title on the outside of the cafe. The restaurant was spelled "RESTURANT."

Maybe this was added class needed in a frontier community.

THE SLOW DROP

The elevation above sea level at High Level is 1,065 feet. Just north of High Level begins the Meander River which flows into the Hay River which flows into Great Slave Lake at Hay River, N.W.T. From the Great Slave Lake the water flows into the wide Mackenzie River which empties into the Arctic Ocean near Tuktoyaktuk.

Incredibly, the water just north of here travels 1,065 miles and drops in elevation a 1,065 feet, onc foot in one mile for that distance.

More incredibly, drop a bottle with a note in it into the Bushe River just east of High Level, and that bottle will travel 1,550 miles from the Bushe, to the Boyer, to the Peace, to the Slave River, to Great Slave Lake and then into the Mackenzie to arrive at sea level at the Arctic Ocean.

VISITS TO CARCAJOU

Two beautiful weekends this past summer were spent at one of Alberta's oldest settlements.

The first weekend started at Thompkins Landing, with Cecil and Janet Weber on their jet cruiser "The Old Sow", and the second by crossing the Peace at the farming settlement of Carcajou.

Carcajou, located on the east side of the Peace River dates back over 100 years as a river stop-over between Fort Vermilion

The M.B. "The Beaver" of O'Sullivan and Stigsen operating on the Peace River up to 1946.

and Peace River and is located almost due east of Keg River Cabins.

Muriel Stigsen came to Carcajou in 1920 and Ted came in 1932 with his parents to take over the trading post.

Carcajou has got to be one of the prettiest settings in Alberta. The townsite is 30-40 feet above the river and the land has a gentle slope to the east.

The buildings are nearly all log, some as old likely as 75 years. The buildings are in good repair for their age; many such as the old Trading Post closed in 1939. The roofs don't leak and the floors are sound.

From the Stigsen's yard one can look up river of the townsite to see cabins, the sadly neglected cemetery with its wooden fences around the graves; the old school, and tucked in the bush is the church.

What history there is here and much history is in the man Ted Stigsen, who was the partner in boating operations of O'Sullivan and Stigsen.

No more can we travel on the M.B. "The Beaver", but we can be glad to chat with the Stigsen's and maybe, if honoured, enjoy the best buttermilk pancakes in the world.

Here is Ted Stigsen's recipe for Buttermilk Pancakes as made at Carcajou:

- 4 cups flour
- 4 cups real buttermilk
- 2 tablespoons sugar
- 1 teaspoon soda
- ½ teaspoon salt
- 3 eggs - or as many as you like.

METHOD:

Mix flour, sugar, salt together and put into a big bowl, add buttermilk and eggs. Mix the soda into a ¼ cup of buttermilk before adding to batter. If batter is too thick, add more buttermilk. On the griddle use a 4 x 4 inch strip of bacon to grease the griddle.

- they are great!

Here is the boating schedule of sailings of M.B. "The Beaver" for 1946 which was the last year they ran.

O'SULLIVAN & STIGSEN
River Transportation Service
and
Winter Trucking Service

SCHEDULE OF SAILINGS of M.B. "The Beaver"
1946
Master: J. P. O'Sullivan
Leaves Peace River Town By-Weekly
5 p.m. Saturdays for:

Ft. Vermilion	April 27	Ft. Vermilion	July 20
Ft. Vermilion	May 11	Ft. Vermilion	Aug. 3
Ft. Vermilion	May 25	Ft. Vermilion	Aug. 17
Ft. Vermilion	June 8	Ft. Vermilion	Aug 31
Ft. Vermilion	June 22	Ft. Vermilion	Sept. 14
Ft. Vermilion	July 6	Ft. Vermilion	Sept. 28

Freight Rates per Cwt.

Vermilion Chutes and Judd's Landing 65c; Fort Vermilion and North Vermilion 55c; Ward's Landing 55c; LaCrate Landing 50c; Carcajou, Keg River, Metis, Tompkin's Landing, Anderson and Monias Creek Landings 40c; Loitgaarden and Battle River 35c; Keppler's Landing 30c Dennison's Landing and points south 25c. Special or flagged stops 50.

Minimum charge on general parcels 25c

Note Marine Risk

We cannot be responsible for any loss of cargo, including livestock, except that due directly to negligence on our part. Insurance may be procured by any shipper from our agent in Peace River at a reasonable rate. Or for a 30% increased freight rate will assume all liability for delivering all cargo to destination safe and in good condition.

We clear C.O.D. Shipments at Station for a Small Charge

Livestock Shippers Read Reverse Side

Passenger Rates

Single Fare $6.00; Meals if Requested 50c Each; Berth $1.00 per night. Return Ticket First Class, Meals and Berth Included, Approximately $30.00.

NOTE—National Revenue Transport Tax of 15% Extra on all tickets.

We Operate Under Passenger License of Province of Alberta.

For Further Information Contact Our Agents
PALACE TRANSFER, PEACE RIVER, ALTA.
Phone 7 or 7
Write us for information re Winter Trucking Service

Shipping Instructions
For Livestock Shippers

We wish to thank the livestock shippers for their co-operation complying with the shipping instructions set forth last season. However, the same drastic conditions as last year still exist to as great an extent if not more so, due mostly to the shortage of feed for the stock. We therefore ask you to please continue to comply with the shipping instructions which follow, as you did last season. There is considerable talk that due to building of the highway from Grimshaw to Great Slave lake the contractors will be shipping by boat on a large scale; we want to assure you insofar as we are concerned we will take care of our regular trade first, than haul what we can of the extra freight, if any.

1. Shippers MUST notify us at least 14 DAYS previous to shipping date. Notice MUST be in writing, giving approximate number of stock to be shipped and trip to be shipped on. Signature of shipper must be signed to notice.

2. Shippers wishing to cancel previous shipping notice MUST NOTIFY US IN WRITING AT LEAST 14 DAYS PREVIOUS TO BOOKING DATE.

Notice cards are available at Post Office, Rankin's Store, Kidd's Store and Porter's Pool Room, Fort Vermilion; at Dodwell's Store, North Vermilion. PLEASE MAIL CARDS DIRECT TO US, DELIVER TO PURSER ON OUR BOAT OR SEND TELEGRAM TO US IN PEACE RIVER.

LIVESTOCK SHIPPING RATES

Cattle $3.00 per head	Hogs $1.00 per head
Sheep 75c per head	Horses $4.00 per head

NOTE MARINE RISK ON FRONT

These prices apply regardless of weight, age or loading point, or whether going up or down the river, except sucking calves shipped with their mothers which are shipped free of charge if under 12 weeks and not over 300 lbs.

Shippers must supply ample feed for livestock for feeding stock on boat to destination, otherwise arrangements must be made with us to supply feed at cost at least 14 days before shipping date.

Any shipper arriving at our boat with stock to ship who has not given us 14 days notice of his proposed shipment does so at his own risk of having to take the stock home to await shipment on the next boat trip.

O'Sullivan & Stigsen
River Transportation Service
Peace River, Alta.

A CHRISTIAN FRIEND

One of the grandest old gents ever to arrive in this part of the country is Adolphus Ghostkeeper of Paddle Prairie. He was born at old Grouard.

In 1939, he started out to move from Manning with three teams and five cows, also three colts. There was no highway but only a cut line to Keg River. The "prairie" had no name.

We admire this man as a man who loves his family, his friends and is a true Christian.

He relates that the first time he travelled to Eleske for the

Prayer in Cree

ᓄᑕᐄᐧᓈ ᑭᒋᑭᓯᑯᐧ ᐁᔮᔮᐣ
ᐱᑕᐦ ᒥ ᐁᐧᔮᒋᑳᑌᐧ ᑭᐄᐧᔨᐄᐣ
ᐱᑕᐦ ᐅ ᒋᒋᐸᔮ ᑭᑎᐯᔮᒋ ᑫᐄᐣ
ᑳᐃᓯ ᓈ ᑐᑕᑲᐄᐧ ᔮᐣ ᑭᓯᑰᐧᐱᑕᐦ
ᐁᑯᓯ ᐃᓯ ᐊᐄᐣ ᑭᑕᐣᑲᒥ

ᐊᐧᓇ- ᑲᑭᓯᑳᐧ ᒥᔮᓈ ᓂᐸᑫᐧ
ᓯᑲᓂᒥ ᓈᒥᓇ ᑕᑕᐤᐠ ᑭᓯᑲᑭ
ᑲᐃᓯ ᑲᓯᓇᒪ ᐊᐧᑭᓈ ᑲᑭᒪᒋ
ᑐᑕᑯᔭᑳᐧᐤ ᐁᑯᓯ ᐃᐧ ᐃᓯᑲᓯᓇᒪ
ᐃᐧ ᓈ ᑲᑭᒪᒋᑐᑕᑳ ᐱᓯᐠ ᑫᔾᒥᓈ
ᐱᒋ ᐁᑲᒪᒋᒪᒥᑐᐦᑐᔭᑕᒫ ᐃᔨᑲ
ᑌᓇᒪ ᐄᐧᓈ ᑲᒪᔭᑖ ᐱᑐᐦ
ᐁᑯᓯ ᐃᑭ

Adolphus Ghostkeeper

pilgrimage, there were only two small buildings at High Level and that's all. That was in 1950.

The first mass at Eleske was at 8 o'clock in the morning, second mass was at 11 o'clock in the morning and the Way of the Cross at 2 o'clock. Some families came by truck, some with teams. "We went with Teddy Martineau and sat in the back of the truck with our bedding," said Adolphus. "Before we left Paddle Prairie Teddy was working in the blacksmith shop with the steel hammer." "Two small pieces of steel hit him in his eyes and he couldn't get them out so he went to Doctor Mary Jackson at Keg River where she took out one piece of steel."

"The other piece of steel she couldn't take out because she said it was too deep in the eye, so he wore dark glasses."

"When we arrived at the Eleske Grotto we went down to pray and after that Teddy got up and went to the blessed Virgin Mary Statue and kneeled down and kissed the dirt."

"Teddy came again where I was praying with him."

"After everything was over, we were going home to Paddle Prairie in the back of the truck and we were chatting. About one mile from Eleske, Teddy said to me, "The steel has come from my eyes," - he took off his glasses and put them in his pocket."

Mr. Ghostkeeper concludes, "This was truly a miracle and I saw it happen with my very own eyes."

The Record-Gazette

Santa letter contest winner

Dear Santa

I have allways wanted a real horse. If you cann't give me one I want my cat to have kittens. If my cat doesn't have kittens. I want a little puppy. If you cann't get me a puppy. I want a little monkey. Can you get me one of these our something else? That will suit a 8 year old girl. Well I better say good bey.

Love Becky Reid

Box 509 High Level

From The Record Gazette, Peace River, Alberta. Christmas, 1974.

AN OLD ENGLISH PRAYER

This verse was included in a letter from friends Gerry and Phyllis Toner. The Toners lived in High Level from 1965 to 1972 and are now at Watson Lake in the Yukon.

Give us, Lord a bit o' sun,
A bit o' work and a bit o' fun;
Give us in all the struggle and sputter
Our daily bread and a bit o' butter;
Give us health, our keep to make,
An' a bit to spare for others' sake;
Give us, too, a bit of song
And a tale, and a book to help us along.
Give us, Lord, a chance to be
Our goodly best, brave wise and free,
Our goodly best for ourself, and others,
Till all men learn to live as brothers."

TLOC - MOI

According to Chief Harry Chonkolay and his wife, Elizabeth, the settlement now called High Level was "Tloc-Moi" which means "Hay Meadow."

The Chonkolays state that, "Tloc-Moi was only a stopping place between Hay Lakes and Fort Vermilion for trappers on their way to and from the trading posts situated at the Fort or Meander River."

Sheridan Lawrence Ranch House upriver and across from Fort Vermilion just before it was torn down in 1968.

"With the help of the Government, and also of intelligent, adventurous and far-seeing men, the travels in this part of the country were greatly improved. Let us mention the late Stubb Lapp and Sheridan Lawrence who hired Indian people to cut a wagon trail from here to Hay Lakes at their own expense to better supply our people with food and necessities."

Harry and Elizebeth pay tribute to Jimmy Jones and Don Staples who in 1950, back from the war, ventured to open the first restaurant here with cabins and garage with basic supplies.

"As times get better," the Chonkolays continue, "we shall remember Johnny Bourassa who flew trappers and sick people from Hay Lakes to Fort Vermilion or Meander River. Let us men-

Chief Harry Chonkolay and his wife Elizabeth of the Slave Band of Upper Hay.

tion also the first settlers like Herman Moormann and a few others who strived to open this vast farm land.''

''These feats, my friends, we ought never to forget,'' the Chonkolays conclude.

THE FARMING POTENTIAL

A recent government body, it is claimed, released figures which show that it is likely that there are over eleven million acres of potentially arable land in the area east of High Level.

By comparison, this is the total of all the farmland under cultivation in the province of Manitoba.

EARLY HIGH LEVEL FOLKS

While history is being made everyday in our area it's fun to turn back time to read an account of the days when High Level was in its infancy. Such an account is related here by now retired teacher Agnes Backstrom. Agnes still lives on the farm east of High Level.

''When my husband Eric, a son Rodney, and a daughter Shirley all took homesteads in the High Level area, I decided to accept Mr. Jardines's offer to teach there. So in August of 1958, my younger son Duane and I moved here.''

''The teacherage, a large trailer, was just off the highway against a beautiful spruce grove. It stood between the school and the garage and cafe owned by Bob and Olga Wallace and Bob Broughton. Olga was never too busy for a friendly chat or helpful plan for the school, despite her very busy life. South of the school were Mrs. Gray at the Blue Top Motel, Mrs. Andy Mathison, the Postmistress and Albert McClarty, the Imperial Oil agent. Through the bush to the west was the sawmill owned by Manford Nelson and Leno Salvador.''

High Level Service Station and Blue Top Lodge, 1958.

Bobby and Valle Gray, Christmas, 1957 at the Blue Top Lodge.

High Level School Class, June, 1959. Back Row: L to R: Dewey Backstrom, Evelyn Moormann, Francis DeWindt, Barry DeWindt, Teacher Agnes Backstrom. Next Row: Rosemary Moormann, Ann Wallace, Skipper Shannon, Bruce Gibb, Murray Shannon, Linda Wilson, Birdie Matheson, Gayle Shannon, Gordon Swanson, Danny Dube. Next Row: Ida Shannon, Laverne Houle, Tommy Shannon, Danny DeWindt, Lewis Moormann. Front Row: Beryl Wallace, Marilyn Bachand, Lawrence Shannon. Missing that day: Viola Swanson.

"The one-roomed school had about twenty pupils coming from the village, the sawmill and the farms to the east. The first while I had three grade nine pupils but these were transferred to Rocky Lane after a while, due to lack of books."

"The people in the area were friendly. Before Christmas they put on a bingo to raise money for Christmas treats for all the district children. Foremost in this venture were John and Gladys Gibb."

"Later the school club showed films from the National Film Board, once a week with Bruce Gibb running the projector. The collection taken was used to buy library books. Everyone came and enjoyed themselves."

"The next spring a Community Club was formed, a sports grounds purchased north of town, and in July a two day sports was put on. They had ball games, games of chance and dancing on an open-air pavilion. John and Gladys Gibb, Chester "Turkey" Brown and Herman Moormann took charge and "made things hum." Everyone in the community pitched in and made these sports a success."

"Late the next winter (1959-60) they organized a drama club. The Shannons, Bachands, Gibbs, Moormanns, Deitrichs, Lambeths and Mr. Brown were among the enthusiastic actors who put on a concert in the spring, the proceeds going towards more books, etc. for the school."

"When the new highway came through and more people moved to High Level, these community activities gave way to others, but I will never forget the kindliness, helpfulness and friendship of these "Old-Timers of High Level."

THE FISH POACHER

A sometimes loud and boisterous gent in High Level — especially boisterous and fun-loving when he has a few snorts under his belt, is Paddy Richards. This man has travelled all over the world and has chosen High Level as his latest, and we hope, last home.

Paddy was born in Nova Scotia. His father was a Sea Captain of Irish descent and his mother was a Micmac Indian.

Tales of his exploits are told on him, one of which is that he and a couple of friends were poaching fish on Slave Lake.

They had lifted their nets and put their catch into gunny sacks when they saw a boat on the horizon. It was obvious to them that it was the Fish and Game Officer. Both boats were familiar figures on the lake.

Quickly they attached a rope to the two gunny sacks of fish and onto the other end of the rope they attached another gunny sack which contained 20 lbs. of very coarse stock salt. The whole batch they threw overboard, attaching the load to a small hook underside of the boat.

The officer in his boat arrived and the crews chatted of the weather and waves as Paddy's crew feigned a peaceful fishing trip with their rods and reels in hand, and their lines out a few feet from the innocent looking boat.

After ordinary chit-chat across the water the officer moved on.

Slowly, and on toward dark the salt in the sack melted easing the weight. They lifted their load on board and headed for shore where they very discreetly disposed of their contraband.

Paddy laughs heartily when he is trapped into listening to the story on himself.

THE DANCES

"The dances we used to have at the old High Level Community Hall were the best in the world. Remember the John Sokoloski orchestra - weren't they great?" This was the comment of former High Level resident, Shirley Brooks, now of Hay River, N.W.T.

As seen by Sharon Percy. HIGH LEVEL MOSQUITOES.

THE MAN IN THE GLASS

Daniel Reid went out to Saint Mary's Boys' School in Edmonton for the 1973 - '74 school term where he took Grade ten. One of the Fathers who taught in the school was Father H. Danielson who sent Dan the following verse in October, 1974.

When you get what you want in your struggle for self
  And the world makes you king for a day,
Just go to a mirror and look at yourself
  And see what THAT man has to say.

For it isn't your father or mother or wife
  Who judgment upon you must pass;
The fellow whose verdict counts most in your life
  Is the one staring back from the glass.

Some people may think you a straight-shootin' chum
And call you a wonderful guy,
But the man in the glass says you're only a bum
If you can't look him straight in the eye.

He's the fellow to please, never mind all the rest,
For he's with you clear up to the end.
And you've passed your most dangerous, difficult test
If the man in the glass is your friend.

You may fool the whole world down the pathway of life
And get pats on your back as you pass.
But your final reward will be heartaches and tears
If you've cheated the man in the glass.

THE FIRST HIGH LEVEL SPORTS

Looking back over the records of the old High Level Sports Association, it was amazing that so few people could do so much work.

At the first High Level Sports, July 11 and 12, 1959, there was $1,889.68 raised in the community and the population was not much more than fifty. Of course, the farmers came to help and people came for miles.

Money was used for the Sports Ground, the Pavilion and for the beginning of the Community Hall.

THE "RUSSIAN NAVY" OF THE PEACE

An interesting story is told by Mrs. Anna Pidruchney of the arrival in the district of a number of families. Her father was Mike Raychyba.

Mrs. Pidruchney taught school at High Level a few years ago and still does a full day's work on her homestead east of High Level. She winters at Vegreville.

Her story follows:

"The outlook of each post-war year in the 1920's was more bleak than the last. Young people were growing up to find that money was scarce; jobs were hard to find and prices for farm commodities were low. But machinery was high; and farmers began to realize that mortgaging their land to buy machinery was going to be their ruin.

It was not very imperative that Mike Raychyba look for homesteads. He had only one son, who could farm with him on his section of land in Prelate, Saskatchewan. But he had eight daughters, who would eventually have to settle some place. By 1929 his household had managed to send four of the older children away to Saskatoon, to P. Mohyla Institute, to High School. The previous year their eldest daughter, Anna, now a school teacher, had married District Agriculturist William Pidruchney and was settled in Vegreville, Alberta.

However, he heeded the requests of a dozen young men — several were his own nephews — and travelled through northern Saskatchewan, searching for good homestead land. Disillusioned, he decided that they might find something better in the Peace River country: where the Government of Alberta was advertising, "Go West young man, and acquire a homestead of 160 acres for $10.00."

A meeting of about thirty men collected a five-dollar fee among themselves, this money to pay the expenses of a nephew, Alex Gizen, to travel with Mr. Raychyba to Peace River. Because their trip would take them through Vegreville, Mrs. Eva Raychyba would accompany them and they would guest at the christening of their first grandchild, Lillian Iris, now wife of Professor Victor Chanasyk, of Guelph University, Guelph, Ontario.

At McLennan they came upon a road-building crew, working with donkeys through a sea of muskeg mud. They checked out the weekly train schedule and begged permission of the station personnel to ride the railroad tracks to Peace River. Mrs. Raychyba lived in that car, the Dodge Victory 6, for two weeks in Peace River while the men went on to Fort Vermilion by the Hudson Bay boat; as so far they had not seen anything that could be classed as a good homestead. In Fort Vermilion they engaged teams to take them across the river and west, where they saw large forests of poplars. In Buffalo Prairie they came upon large patches of level prairie land ready for the plow. The Land Office in Peace River registered their request. The son remembers that that was the last trip the Dodge Victory 6 made; it had no shock-absorbers and no springs left.

An exodus of twelve young men during the summer of 1930 took some careful planning. In May, which was after seeding in Saskatchewan, two married couples, Mike and Annie Prockiw and Peter and Nastia Chomiak, stopped in Vegreville for the night. The two young women travelled in the back of the three-ton truck, sitting on their trunks wedged amid household freight, under cover of a tarp, while their husbands enjoyed the front seat with Mr. Mike Raychyba.

Mrs. Chomiak, now Mrs. Andrew Sarapuk, relates how a large group of Peace River residents watched them load their freight onto the scow — and advised them to change their minds about travelling with "The Russian Navy." The scow at that time was only a "flat" of heavy lumber propelled by a paddle wheel turned by the truck motor. Mike Raychyba stood in front, measuring the depth of the water with a long poplar tree and Bill Gretchen stood at the back paddling it in line with the front, so that a current would not swing it on a sand bar or out into deep water.

They arrived safely in Fort Vermilion and the hired team deposited them on a homestead fifteen miles east of the present High Level town, this land still owned by young Peter Chomiak. Mike Prockiw's homestead, just south of Jack Gibb, was sold in '74 to the John Gibb family. Both places became Stopping Places for trappers and freighters along the High Level Ridge to the North. Son-in-law William Fedeyko and his wife Justine with their two sons, William and Dennis, own and rent the lands homesteaded by Mr. Mike Raychyba.

Andrew Sarapuk, Nick Hayday, Bill Gretchen, Stanley Slotiuk, Mrs. Michael (Mary) Panko, and Mrs. Stanley (Irene) Lawrence are some names of this early group whose presence is still noted in this district.

Now other pioneers and newcomers availed themselves of "Mike's" freighting service. In later years Mr. Raychyba would be greeted by strangers who would shake his hand and say, "You probably don't remember me, but you freighted me down the Peace River with my twin boys and my seven black horses." "I don't recognize you, but I can never forget you," reminisces Mr. Raychyba. "I have seen many horses, but I have never come across any as beautiful as those of yours. Black as night, and as identical as seven black marbles. And I worried about those six-year-old twin boys, how they would fare among the mosquitos and wolves without a mother." "God was with us. Both boys are married, have families, and are not too far from each other, so that I visit with each one every few weeks."

Mike Raychyba kept enlarging his scow till it boasted a large eating-sleeping shelter in its mid-section. He was on the river till the summer of 1938, when he set it up as housing for his wife and five daughters, who had left the Saskatchewan home to the now-married son and moved out to the Peace River Flats just north of the bridge, to be with Father in 1937. This acreage is still owned by daughter Irene. The last two years on the boat were comfortable and happy ones. At his request daughter Mary came on board as chief clerk and cook. Her happy disposition coupled with organization of the business and her ability to make a tasty soup from anything and almost nothing, endeared her to everyone who crossed her path. "The perfume of freshly-baked bread still lingers over the miles of The Mighty Peace River," claim her passengers.

For the family of Grandfather Theodore Raychyba and his wife Justina, this would be the second homesteading exodus in Canada; from Ukraine they had settled in Gimli, Manitoba; from Gimli in ten years they had migrated to better lands in Prelate, Saskatchewan; and now he wanted to see these recent homesteads. In June of 1932, as they slept in their tent on the bank of the Peace River, Grandmother died — quietly in her sleep. Her son, Michael Raychyba, had no other choice . . . she is buried in the Peace River Cemetery. Beside her, later, is buried her granddaughter, Katerena Olga Raychyba, who passed away in 1946. Grandfather spent the winter with the Peter Chomiak family, then returned to complete his days with the Michael Raychyba household in Prelate, Saskatchewan. He died in 1935.

When the children left home, Mrs. Raychyba spent the summers with her husband on the homesteads, where they almost completed a new house on a full cement basement; that house is still in use now. By this time Andrew Sarapuk's General Store, butcher shop, gasoline tanks and general trade in farm products was also appointed as — Rocky Lane Post Office —. The "Boys" had done well. Mr. and Mrs. Raychyba could take time to visit, and to bask in the grateful appreciation of these families.

In 1954, as they arrived at home from a visit with the Bohay families, where she had read the Ukrainian Voice to the gathering of neighbours, (this was a weekly enjoyment) she collapsed — and died three weeks later in the Fort Vermilion Hospital. She is buried in the Peace River Cemetery.

Mike Raychyba kept on farming his Rocky Lane homesteads, and spent his winters with his son-in-law Michael Panko and daughter Mary in St. Michael, Alberta, where he died in January, 1970. He is buried in the Evergreen Memorial Gardens, Edmonton."

OIL BIDS IN 1967

Bidding was high for Crown reserve sale of petroleum and natural gas leases in 1967. The largest single bid in one sale in April was for $1,971,200.00 for a 320 acre parcel in the Zama North Area by the Royal Trust Company. In the adjacent township at the

Sign Posts, Oil Boom Days. Meander River turn off to Zama. March, 1967.

same sale Texaco Exploration and Texaco Canada Ltd. combined to pay $5,533,817.00 for 320 acre parcels in sections 25, 26, 35 and 36.

O.K., GOODBYE

Listen as any of your friends or neighbors in this area are talking on the phone and sure as guns the conversation will always end the same.

Yes, be it the conversation in the language of the Beaver, the Cree, or the Slavey; the Low German of the Mennonites; the Ukrainian or the Polish of Rocky Lane; the French; the English; or any other, the end will always be the same "O.K., Goodbye."

A HOMESTEADER'S LOGIC

The following appeared in the Northern Advocate of Manning in June of 1966:

"A homesteader is a recluse who chooses his self-imposed exile with its accompanying lack of restrictions rather than the stresses and strains of competition demanded in order to exist in an organized society. He contributes nothing to the world at large, there being no community in which to serve. He retains and uses for his own comfort and ease, the medicines, machines, literature and music developed by that same society which he rejects and which he cannot live entirely without."

"Incongruously, progress is measured in terms of roads, power lines, telephones and schools, etc. Such creeping innovations of civilization are then received with welcoming arms as a child of his loins, a product of his own creation, a result of his own sweat and determination - ones with which he is able to cope having first conceived the plans, drawn up the blueprints and supervised the building of it personally."

"And then — when it is too late, he realizes that he has spawned a monster identical to that from which he cunningly escaped years earlier."

O.M.J. — THE SUPER SALESMAN

How would you like to loan $250,000.00 to a homesteader 500 miles north of Edmonton? He has a half section cleared and part of another half section broke.

Actually he doesn't want the $250,000.00 for his homestead. He wants to build a hotel at a stopping place on the Mackenzie Highway. No; there's no railroad into it yet but it will come. No; there is no industry in it yet except a 2-3 million foot sawmill, but it will come. No; there are only about fifty people there, but more will come. No; the farmers don't stop in High Level because they have to take their grain out to Manning or Grimshaw, but there will be elevators if there is a railroad built. No; the oil industry

The start of construction of the High Level Hotel in the spring of 1963. Right to Left: Shorty MacDonald, Wally Klak, Hans Bolton, Owen Jordan, and Emil Sherbaniuk.

doesn't stop in High Level much, but they will if our town goes ahead.

These would have been answers that a very determined Owen Jordan must have given to the outside world when he made up his mind that this part of the country needed an up-to-date stopping place with real running water.

What did he and his wife, Fanny, offer as security? Well, the homestead, the 7 unit crude diesel heated cabins with a bed and wash basin for furnishings; the garage which was under pending sale, and a wee general store 30' x 35'; the 10 stool, 4 table cafe; a small cat, but mainly - a look of grim determination.

This was the summer and fall of 1962 and by the following spring the foundation was commenced for a hotel which would include 34 rooms, a bar, a restaurant, a bank, and a bus depot. A huge undertaking for a homesteader and his hard working wife.

It was a mountain rising out of the prairie to see that 20,000 ft. building being created during the summer of 1963. It was, and looked enormous surrounded by the small store, the 16' x 20' double cabins, and Mrs. Jordan's ever busy "Laundry" which was a simple granary 14' x 16', with two washing machines and a dryer all smelling strong of laundry soap and bleach. On the north side of the hotel were three or four small shacks.

Work progressed rapidly as there was good weather that summer, and with a huge crowd the official opening took place on

February 4th, 1964 with a standing room only program.

With the only bar in an area 120 miles south or 200 miles north, with modern rooms and with a good restaurant it was apparent that the Jordans had sold financiers on a good project. It gave High Level a security link as a distributing centre.

GOODBYE TO THE FERRY

In September, 1974 a beautiful new bridge was opened across the Peace River at Fort Vermilion, ending a period of semi-isolation fall and spring each year.

True to her pioneering spirit and her love of poetry, Mrs. Elizabeth Ward Rivard wrote a poem bidding farewell to the ferry. The poem is dedicated to Archie Mercredi and all the men who worked to give so many years of service on the ferry.

Good-bye dear old ferry
We don't need you anymore,
They have built us a bridge
Right across from shore to shore.

You have given us faithful service
Thru summer days and night,

The Ferry "Fort Vermilion" making its pass under the new bridge on September 19, 1974 on its final run at Fort Vermilion. On board besides the piper is long time ferryman John Gronvall, Vic Yeomens, and Ferry Inspector Al Dittman. In the car is Mrs. Gronvall, and daughters Carey Lee and Carman. Operating the ferry is Arthur Lizotte. Photo by Miss Louise Wiens, LaCrete.

From the dodging of the driftwood
Till the coming of the ice.

Oh yes, you've had your troubles
When the engine wouldn't start,
And folks waited on the river bank
Feeding skeeters all the night.

In future years how will we know
When the seasons change about,
With no one to put the ferry in
And no one to take her out.

May you find a shining river
Where the sky is always blue,
So good-bye dear old ferry
And the best of luck to you.

1916 Case 65 H.P. Steam Engine which was originally brought into the area in 1939 by river boat on the Peace River by Sheridan Lawrence. Used later by Ward and Rivard, and now owned by Henry Harvey Peters of LaCrete. On board is, left to right, Jacob H. Peters, Henry Harvey Peters, John Ward and waving Stanley Smith. Picture taken by Miss Louise Wiens of LaCrete at the opening of the bridge at Fort Vermilion on September 19, 1974.

MACKENZIE ROAD TO BE BUILT

From the Peace River Record Gazette comes the information that on February 19, 1939 the final sanction was given by Hon. T.

A. Crearer, Minister of Natural Resources, to construct a winter traction road connecting the Peace River division of the Northern Alberta Railways with Great Slave Lake, almost 400 miles further north. "This will be the greatest roadway of its kind in Canada. It will serve the purpose of a railway and tractors drawing ten or more trailers will ply along it.

Department officials expect that next year the pitchblend concentrates from Eldorado mines, gold concentrates from the Yellowknife mines and the fish from Great Slave Lake will be hauled to the railway over this road.

At the same time announcement of Ottawa's approval was given, announcement of the route was made public as follows:

From Meikle river (The Third Battle) the road will run straight north to Keg River. In this fifty mile stretch the road will not follow the telegraph line.

Leaving Keg River the road will follow the telegraph line a distance of about eighty miles to a point east of Watt Mountain.

From this point a thirty mile stretch of the road will end up ten miles east of Upper Hay River post.

The last piece of road about 130 miles in length will cross the Hay River to Lower Hay River post and continue to Great Slave Lake.

The proposed road from a point near Alexandra Falls to Providence is a Federal project, and must be carried out by the senior government if and when it is decided to do so, which will not likely be this year."

It is interesting to note that there is no High Level mentioned in this report.

Father M. Jal at High Level on his way from Fort Vermilion to Habay. March, 1947.

A THOUGHT

Here is a little quotation made by Father M. Jal as he left High Level in June, 1966 for Belgium.

"No matter what your faith,
love your fellow man."

THE NEW LAND

In June of 1962, Marilyn Bachand won the Chamber of Commerce prize for a new slogan for the High Level District. That slogan is "The New Land."

SANTA AT HIGH LEVEL

Probably one of the happiest times for children in the early stages of growth of High Level was the grand arrival of Santa Claus at Reid's Super "A".

A variety of means used by old St. Nick to arrive in town added to the suspense. Sid Quist always had something to do with the arrangements.

There are not very many around who can remember his arrival in 1963 in the back of Tony's Truck. The truck backed up to the front door of the store, the doors were flung open and out the old boy jumped with his "Ho, Ho, Ho."

The little store on the highway was jam packed with happy kids and their parents. He had a few minutes to spend with each child for there were not more than eighty in the district.

The grandest show occurred in December, 1966 when at about 50 degrees below Santa chose to arrive by helicopter.

Roy Hanson, Town Manager, wrote to his friends and described the event like this:

"On Saturday, December 17, 1966 there was a large gathering on main street in front of Reid's Super "A" Foods. The active flow of traffic was stopped in the entire block awaiting the expected visitor; and the chill wind of the afternoon failed to dampen the spirits of the youngsters or older folks. Suddenly from the north a blinking light appeared, approaching rapidly, making a circle over the crowd; and, amidst a dense cloud of swirling, powdery snow as the object came to rest, Santa Claus emerged from the helicopter with all the glory surrounding such a spectacle."

"The nature of his call was to answer Gordon Reid's invitation to meet the kiddies, and it is only natural that Santa would save the reindeer for the long run on Christmas Evening."

Santa days that year saw 580 kids arrive and 1967 was the last year for Santa at the store when there were just under 800 children to sit on his knee. Fire regulations would not permit it to be continued in 1968.

THE ELESKE GROTTO

A simple person who is filled with mercy, charity and love of God is Father Cesaire Mariman, long time priest of our area.

He told of the building of the beautiful grotto at Eleske, 25 miles from Fort Vermilion towards High Level on the Child Lake Reserve.

The doctor at Fort Vermilion held little hope for the long life of any of the Beaver Indians on the reserve for he said they were germ-filled with T.B.

Father decided to build a grotto dedicated to Saint Bernadette because she was the Patron Saint of the Eleske Territory. It was hoped that the prayers at the grotto would cure any kind of sickness, especially T.B.

It was just after the second world war and there was no money but they were given a few sacks of old cement which was already stone-like by Jimmy Jones at High Level.

"We started smashing it, first with an axe and with a hammer and with a heel," says Father Mariman.

They went to the neighbourhood settlement and borrowed an oats crusher from farmer Andrew Hawryluik but it was too slow.

"I am going to put wings on that oat crusher; my father was a windmill builder in the old country," said Father Mariman to the lad helping him, and with that he made big ladder-shaped wings.

They were tired but that evening when they had mounted the machine with wings on an old wagon he relates that there came a strong breeze as if sent by God to please them, and the windmill

The Eleske Grotto.

started to turn full speed and it was very easy for them to turn all that cement into fine powder.

Andrew Hawryluik along with Alex Bilesky and the Indians of the reserve worked hard gathering steel and rocks and trees, making cement and building the flooring and part of the walls.

As they neared the end of the construction of the main part of the structure, Andrew said to Father, "You should go in full speed with the horses to Fort Vermilion and get at least three sacks of good cement, three and one half would be better. We need to be able to fill up that hole in the vault of the dome of the grotto."

"I went," said Father, "and found three sacks at Steven's store but then Mr. Stevens said to me," "I have in my warehouse here one sack that is all broken and I am going to give it to you as a present." Father said, "That is Providential for that three and one half sacks is exactly what we need to make extra good cement."

Back to Eleske they went and soon the men had finished the main structure, and David Courtoreille did the very fine work on part of the lateral walls supporting the so-called, "Way of the Cross," and so now we have the Eleske Grotto.

THEIR FRIENDS

Things were going well for Gordon and Edna Reid in the store business. The business had grown from the first little general store of 400 square feet in 1963, to the second one of 800 square feet, to the new one opened in August 1974 with a whopping 2,500 square feet. Even this by 1966 was not enough for an oil boom had hit High Level. Plans were made to build another new store beside the existing one.

The weekend of April 9th, 1967 was a busy one. Oil camps were paying well, oil workers earning big money and their families were eating well. By Saturday night the Reids had put $21,000 into their old J.J. Taylor safe. Much of this had come in Saturday from oil company head offices in Calgary.

At 2:00 A.M. April 10th, men cut a hole into the warehouse behind the store, crawled in and tore the safe apart.

The assistant manager of the store, Gerry Toner, found this mess Monday morning. He found utter disaster in the form of smashed desks, papers all over the floor, but worst of all he found the safe destroyed. Gerry summoned Gordon who called the police.

Here was a young operation in the north up to its ears in debt, with a $21,000 loss none of which Reids could actually call their own; none was insured. The culprits had taken all cash and cheques except $136.00 which had been carelessly left scattered on the floor. A payroll was to be met, within hours there was a $13,000 overdraft at the bank and it seemed bankruptcy was inevitable. The store remained closed all day.

At the front door of Reid's Store after the break in of April 10, 1967.

Tuesday morning the store opened with the $136.00 in the till.

About 9:30 A.M. Peter Machura and Owen Jordan came to the store, picked up Gordon and took him home for coffee which Edna had prepared. Pete announced that the community had decided to take up a collection and send the Reids away on a holiday to forget the ordeal for awhile. Edna cried and thanked them but said, "No, this is no time to escape from reality, the situation is far too serious."

Before the second cup of coffee Peter said, "You know, Gordon and Edna, this isn't really why we are here. The real reason is that in my shirt pocket I have a paper and on it is a list of twenty-one people in the area who have signed a note for $1,000 each at the bank to keep you going."

Here we have twenty-one friends either struggling farmers, new businessmen, workers in the oil business, mill workers, or whoever who have faith enough in them to risk $1,000 each for friendship.

Where in the world could you find such friends as Gordon and Edna have? Nowhere but in this new frontier.

Yes, it did indeed keep them from foreclosure and to this day Gordon and Edna have never seen this list, nor do they ever want to.

They want to believe that whoever of the old-timers they meet, had to be one of those who helped.

HOT & COLD

On April 28th, 1975 High Level was the warm spot in Alberta at 14 degrees C., but also was the cold spot in Alberta at -2 degrees. Again, on April 29th, the next day High Level was warm spot in Alberta at 13 degrees C., and cold spot in Alberta at -4 degrees.

High Level January, 1954 with Cafe, Cabins and Garage.

GROWTH

Mick and Naida Watson came to High Level on June 8th, 1959 to homestead east of town.

Mick had worked seismic here in 1953 and was impressed with the country.

In 1964, after the railroad had been here for a year, Naida wrote a little poem giving credit to the growth of the town. Here it is:

Come sit awhile and remember
that five years ago,
there wasn't even an ember
of how our town would grow.

The new Mackenzie Highway is here,
It runs on north near main street,
Many a new business seem to appear,
From nowhere they come to compete.

A new hotel just opened its doors,
To serve the district for miles around.
It isn't like it was before,
My, how our town grows by leaps and bounds.

What is to be Main Street, High Level in May, 1964. Judy's Ready-to-wear is the only building on main street. It is now the Echo Office.

Construction of Main Street High Level 1964. Looking west.

The law is here, the banks are too,
We have churches and a new school.
Don't know where the credit is due
But I think the railway supplied the fuel.

THE BIG PLATEAU

In the early days of travel in the area, when freighters came up from Fort Vermilion to the big plateau, then down north to the

Burning brush on Fahlman's lot. Left Leno Salvador; Right Roy Harbourne 1964.

Hay River or across to Hay Lakes, there was a stopping place on the big plateau.

That point was called High Level.

OUR GRAND OLD COWBOY

If we ever have a museum in our area, one of the most priceless things we could have in it would be one of those big hats of a cowboy who spent a few years around High Level. Our cowboy

Cache owned by Trader George Clarke near High Level about 1933. Picture of Warren Clarke.

Covered wagon used by Father M. Jal in September, 1946 near High Level en route from Fort Vermilion to Upper Hay and Hay Lakes.

was Jack Chesshir, better known to those who loved him as, "Oregon Jack."

Jack came from Oregon in 1919 to Fairview and moved to Manning in the early 1940's. Off and on he spent time with friends at High Level.

Oregon Jack died on August 16th, 1973 at Autumn Lodge at Berwyn. He would have been eighty on November 14th, 1973.

CHAMPS

Wheat from the Mission Farm at Fort Vermilion took first prize at the Centennial Exhibitions at Philadelphia in 1876 - one hundred years ago, and recently, our George Bruinsma who farms just north of High Level has taken the following prizes at the Calgary Seed Fair:

1966	First	Rapeseed	Arlo
1967	Second	Rapeseed	Arlo
1968	Second	Rapeseed	Arlo
1969	Grand Champion	Rapeseed	Target
1970	Grand Champion	Rapeseed	Arlo
1971	First	Rapeseed	Arlo
1972	First	Rapeseed	Arlo
1972	First	Alfalfa	Vernal
1973	First	Rapeseed	Span
1973	Grand Champion	Alfalfa	Vernal

Of this we are proud.

A winter scene. The new grain elevators and the new sawdust burners at High Level, winter of 1966.

THE COUCH DELIVERY

Books will be written about the career of a true Northern Alberta Pioneer, Dr. Laura Margaret Attrux.

Hundreds of babies were delivered in thirty-five years, nearly always in homes but occasionally in her office.

One night she got a loud rap on her door about 10:30 P.M. When she opened the door there stood a little fellow about five years old. "Nurse," he said "My Mom's going to have her kid and my dad's drunk." "O.K.," Laura said, "Tell your Mom I'll be there."

Away she went to the edge of town with her black bag picking up her friend Edna Reid on the way.

Sure enough there was the mother in labour, and sure enough there was Dad sound asleep and drunk as blazes on the Winnipeg couch - the only bed in the house.

They stoked the fire, put on a tub of water to heat, cleaned the chimneys on both coal oil lamps and began the task of "readying the delivery room". First they had to remove Dad from the couch. Laura and Edna gently picked him up and slid him lengthways under the couch and in three minutes they could hear him snoring.

Mother was then prepared for delivery on the couch, and in about an hour they had delivered a fine, young baby boy.

ONLY 280 MILES FROM THE ELEVATORS

For twenty-five years the Gibbs farmed at Buffalo Head Prairie forty miles south of Fort Vermilion. Until 1950 they shipped all farm products up river to Peace River or sold it locally.

With the completion in 1948 of the Mackenzie Highway and the Fort Vermilion road, they were able to haul grain forty miles north to Fort Vermilion crossing on the ferry there, fifty miles west to High Level and 180 miles south to Grimshaw. This was big progress.

Gladys Gibb relates that her first sight of High Level was in 1950 when she accompanied husband John to Peace River by truck. At that time there was a Dept. of Highways Building and yard at High Level.

The Gibbs moved to their High Level farm in 1955 to live on land they homesteaded in 1952. The thought that they could be 190

A familiar landmark. The John Gibb farmstead east of High Level along the Fort Vermilion road.

miles from the grain elevators rather than 280 miles appealed to them.

The roads, she tells, were very narrow and one of the problems was the spring flooding of the Bushe River east of High Level. In 1957 the bridge was washed out and the Dept. of Highways had to put in a barge for a time so that mail, groceries, gas, etc., could be carried across the river for the settlements of Rocky Lane and Fort Vermilion as well as for the newly established High Level homesteaders.

When the Gibbs moved to their homestead eight miles east of High Level in 1955 they travelled to Andrew Sarapuk's Rocky Lane store for their mail and groceries, and also enjoyed the visit with Sarapuks and whoever happened to be at the store.

The land they homesteaded at High Level, as now, was all bush which had to be cut, piled and burned then plowed. The very tough work followed for years - that of hand picking the roots. There were no machine root pickers.

THE BOOZE THAT AGED

During the renovations of the original store in the spring of 1963 in High Level, it was found that the shaving lined walls upstairs were soggy with water leaking through fine cracks in the asphalt rolled roof. The paper mache walls were torn out, and the shavings were thrown out by scoop shovel from the upstairs window.

Nailed behind one of the sheets of fibreboard, neatly tucked into shavings was an unsealed bottle of Rye whiskey and an unsealed bottle of Gin.

The date on the bottle showed that it came from the Northwest Territories and was dated 1951.

Of course all those years there hadn't been any liquor outlets nearer than Hay River to the north, and Manning or Peace River to the south.

While talking to Jimmy Jones living in 1963 at Steen River, he recalled that an employee of his who was quite a boozer had asked him one time if he had seen two bottles which had been purchased in the North. The fellow admitted that he had hidden the bottles somewhere for fear that Florence, Jimmy's wife would confiscate them.

Jimmy speculated that he had to conceal his extra purchases by very carefully lifting the nails on the fibreboard, then tucking his prize into the shavings, brushed up his mess and fell into a sound and drunken sleep.

Next day, he must have awakened and found that his extra purchases could not be located. Fearing that he be accused of being an alchoholic, he probably presumed that his two bottles had been stolen from him or that they had been taken from him to avoid a second round.

He could not be suspicious of anyone nor could he shake his memory of his own trickery.

He suffered in silence, and his liquor had aged beautifully for twelve years.

A WORKER

A hard working gal, who received little credit for lots of work over the years, is Marge Pietsch.

Marge was long time Secretary-Treasurer of the High Level Sports Association. Without her, it is unlikely that the old Community Hall would have been completed.

70 YEARS MARRIED

Not very many people are as privileged as a few of us were on October 18th, 1975 to have been invited to a 70th Wedding Anniversary.

The old couple, Antoine and Alice Courtorielle, 92 and 86 years old, were married at the settlement of Carcajou on the banks of the beautiful Peace River on August 18th, 1905 and have lived in the area continuously ever since.

Both are extremely healthy and during the course of this great evening kissed each other and told of their courting days.

Five of the couples six children attended. John and his wife and part of their family came from Turin near Lethbridge, David and his wife and family were there, and bustling around all evening were daughters Ester Van Patten and Mary who hosted the evening, daughter Albina Kazonay arrived later. Many of the 82 grandchildren and 89 great-grandchildren attended. Long time friends came from all over.

The night at Rocky Lane began with a supper of turkey, wild goose, moose, bear meat as well as bannock and salad for 80 of the family and friends. About 16 of the couples' long-time friends sat

Antoine and Alice Courtorielle, on their 70th Wedding Anniversary party at the Rocky Lane Hall.

at the room-centered head table with Antoine and Alice.

A little program followed the dinner headed by a prayer in song in Cree by Adolphus Ghostkeeper of Paddle Prairie. Poet Elizabeth Rivard of Fort Vermilion had a poem entitled, "A Long, Long Trail" which was read by Denise Eek of Fort Vermilion. Mrs. Rivard then related a little history of 50 years, knowing the Courtorielles.

Mrs. Liza Paul, admitting to a keen 84, looking beautiful in her 60 year old velvet outfit hauled her mouth organ from her purse and played a "square." Mrs. Paul's feet tapped a rhythm maybe even louder than she played her mouth organ. Everyone roared approval of the little floor show put on when the old couple danced a few steps of a jig.

A round of old-time singing followed ending with "For They are Jolly Good Fellows." We sang songs heard rarely today; songs like "You are my Sunshine" and "Home on the Range."

The old gent rose to his feet after the program and thanked everyone for coming out to say "Hello."

Old-time dancing followed until way on into the night while old friends chatted with Antoine and Alice.

This is a night to be remembered . . .

A NEW FRIEND

Life is interesting when you can look for and find a new friend. A new friend was found in October, 1975 at the Opportunity North Conference in Peace River in character Mrs. Vera Lane of Peace River. Her company was enjoyable, and she offered a poem which she wrote in August called:

REFLECTIONS

And I live here
Where the pine trees sigh,
The moon looks down
From a cloudy sky.

Sees me not
While the wild winds cry,
To rest a moment
As they pass by.

They travel on
The moon, wind and clouds,
While the pines and I
Feel stirred or bowed.

Might I ride
On the wind or cloud,
Or sleep by the pines

Or sing aloud.

Whatever comes
Or is to be,
I feel their presence
Comforts me.

To sit in shade
Or walk in the sun,
In an echoing glade
When day is done.

Then at last
Lie quitely down,
Like needles of pine
When life is done.

THE SCHOOL BUS DRIVER

One of the toughest old birds to homestead in the district was Herman Moormann who came here to file in 1950 and lived on the farm here alone, away from his family at Fairview for three years. His wife, Marjorie, and eight children moved here in 1954.

Herman took time off to visit his many friends amongst the white and native population, and was always ready to help a neighbour homesteader get started. He became the friend and counsellor of many new settlers.

He was responsible for the first school at High Level and the first Catholic church in the district.

Most old-timers remember him though because of his colour-

First High Level School Bus. Owned and operated by Herman Moormann. L. to R. David Friesen, Teacher; Olga Kostiw, Doug Gray 1955-56.

First Class Picture High Level School 1955-56. Back Row, L to R: Hazel Gibb, Gail Gray, Jack Gibb, David Dube, Henry Moormann. Front Row, L to R: Carl Krieger, Evelyn Moorman, Danny Dube, Bruce Gibb. First Teacher Olga Kostiw took the picture.

ful old school bus, the first in the district back in 1955. The few farm kids had to be transported to High Level and Herman had an old van, capacity of twelve maximum, which was used.

The roads were poor, there was no telephone service in the farming area, the heating system in the van was not the most comfortable but the spirit of the driver was an inspiration to the kids who rode in it.

Mr. Moormann passed away on May 26th, 1966 at age 61 after suffering from cancer for two years. He accepted his sufferings and death with the same courage and determination always known of him by others.

THE DOCTOR

What a wonderful thing it was when Dr. Mary Percy Jackson of Keg River was named "Woman of the Year" for 1975, for her devoted service to the Keg River and surrounding area.

BOOZE

We would wonder how many gallons of booze Vic Jordan without grumbling, unloaded at the brand-spanking new bus depot in High Level after it opened in early 1964. There must have been hundreds, for all liquor had to be brought in from Manning or the outside by bus.

Until the hotel opened there was no regular beer outlet in High

A grand couple, Bus Agent Vic Jordan and his wife Ann, atop Watt Mountain in 1966.

Level and until the Liquor store opened in June of 1968 there was no liquor outlet for 120 miles.

THIRTY-SIX YEARS AGO

Immediate activity on the mining road to the north is indicated by reports reaching the Peace River Record Gazette in February, 1939 of a tractor train being outfitted for the trip. Five

First Cat Train to travel north of the Proposed Mackenzie Highway, 1940.

or six tractors, hauling several sleighs will be shipped from Edmonton about March 1st, and will make the overland trip via the winter road, which is expected to be completed by March 31st.

* * *

This road was to become the Mackenzie Highway, which was completed for limited traffic in 1946.

THE ELEVATORS

The first load of grain was delivered to the Alberta Pacific Grain Elevator in High Level by John Gibb on Cash Purchase Ticket No. 417601 on November 2nd, 1964. John delivered 127 bushels of Flax and received $2.95½ per bushel. Art Jacobs, Harry Bannister, George P. Wiebe and Dorothy Boire delivered the next four loads on November 3rd.

Some of those to follow on the 4th were Jimmy Ward, Orval Ryder, Mary Batt, Otto Hartman, Pete Robinson, Stig Dunker and Alex Rygus.

Yes, November 3rd, 1964 was a great day for the area for this was the day of the official opening of the most northerly grain rail shipping point in the world.

Prior to 1945/46 grain had to be shipped by boat, tug, and barge upriver to Peace River. In most cases the grain had to be sacked - this in itself was an expense.

When the Mackenzie Highway was opened in 1946 the farmers rejoiced for they could haul bigger loads by truck the 50 miles from Fort Vermilion to High Level, then 180 miles south to Grimshaw.

The Mackenzie Highway just south of High Level, 1957. Picture by Mrs. V. Gray.

Mackenzie Highway just south of High Level. Spring of 1948. Travel only in the ditch.

Fort Vermilion Road at High Level 1948. Hotel now sits just above Mary Simmons head.

Mrs. E. Ward-Rivard cutting the ribbon for the opening of the elevators at High Level, November, 1964. Front Row: Rod Roth, Gordon Reid, Metro Kowal, Lewis MacRoberts, Mrs. Ward-Rivard, Arthur Simmons, Mike Raychyba.

Now with the opening of the elevators at High Level, it seemed a very simple matter to deliver the grain.

The elevator agent was a High Level homesteader, Doug Rule. Doug had taken out a homestead thirteen miles east of town in 1954 and when the railroad became a possibility or likelihood he went back to work for Alberta Pacific at Grimshaw, transferred to Manning, then on to High Level in 1964.

The farmers from the whole area along with High Level Town and the Chamber of Commerce had a wonderful parade for the opening followed by a luncheon and a dance. Fort Vermilion was asked to pick an old-timer from its area for the ribbon cutting and they chose Mrs. Elizabeth Rivard, long time farmer.

Many tears of joy were shed that day and many yarns were swapped - it was indeed a great day and a great event when our elevators were opened.

THE COYOTE'S LUNCH

The year 1959 saw a new bunch of homesteaders move to the High Level area. One was middle aged, Owen Jordan who by 1966 had cleared the poplar off three hundred and twenty acres of fine farmland and claimed an average crop of sixty bushels per acre. Back in those years his closest neighbours were bears, lynx, wolves, coyotes, moose and deer. He tended to gossip about animals the way some people talk about other people.

"A funny thing happened a few years ago," said Owen in a 1966 chat. "I was combining a wheat field and the noise of the machine sent the field mice running straight into the jaws of a coyote who'd been watching the action. I quit for lunch and when I got back to the combine, there was old Mr. Coyote just lying down waiting for me to chase him up another meal.

Taken from Maclean's - Feb. 19/66.

INDUSTRY HITS HIGH LEVEL

October 19th and 20th, 1957 were big days for High Level. A new business was arriving. The business marked the start of the massive industry that lumber is today in the area.

Marked on the vehicles arriving then was R. A. Craig, Cadomin and with the equipment came owners Manford Nelson and Leno Salvador as well as Billy Grieves, Stig Dunker, Rudy Schwartz, Paul and Pauline Stevens, Joe Mazur, Phillip Ello, and

Manford Nelson in 1957 while he was a partner of High Level Lumber.

Billy Grieves, 1957 of High Level Lumber.

High Level Lumber Planer. Spring of 1958.

brothers Reno and Sylvio Bertoia. Judy Dunbar was to arrive later.

The new company was to be called High Level Lumber Co. and it operated until 1963 on what is now the west edge of the residential area of the town.

The arrival of the railroad brought new operators into the area. Leo Arsenault and his family built a big new sawmill as did the Camille Boucher family. Norm and Bob Benson and Ivan and Lyman Brewster built mills and there were other smaller ones.

The timber in the area is under lease to Swanson Lumber Co.

High Level Ranger Station, a one time hub of activity in the area.

and according to Bob Walters, production will be over 100 million F.B.M. for 1976.

This converted means 2,000 rail cars of lumber or the framing for 10,000 homes.

What a difference from the humble beginning in 1957.

Albert Forest Service. Fire Camp, Footner Lake 1966.

THEIR ARK

A collection of cabins and additions which seemed in 1972 to be tugged together with polythene was the spacious homestead home of friends Alex and Del Orlesky. They lovingly dubbed it, "The Ark."

In October, 1972 forty-four men, women and children gathered at "The Ark" for the first church service of what now has become the Rocky Lane Church.

ONE SCHOOL KID

In June of 1975 Miss Sandy Medynski graduated from the High Level School, Grade 12 Class, and became the first student who started school in High Level, completed all twelve years in the school and graduated from it.

In 1963 when Sandy started school there were just over thirty students enrolled.

"Being the first to complete Grades 1 through 12 at our local school is an honour," stated Sandy.

DR. LAURA

Our friend, Laura Margaret Attrux was born June 28, 1909 at Duck Lake, Saskatchewan and was raised on a prairie-wooded homestead at Hafford, near Battleford. She was the daughter of Joseph and Victoria Attrux who were strict, religious parents who taught her that life was worthwhile wherever there were people.

Times were tough on the prairie homestead and through these tough times this girl got to know the value of hard work coupled with thrift. Laura was an adventurer even in those days.

Early in life she was determined to become a doctor. She studied hard and worked hard but by the time she had completed her high school she had decided to become a nurse.

She enrolled in St. Paul's Hospital in Saskatoon in August, 1927 and graduated as a Registered Nurse in August, 1930. She remained at St. Paul's Hospital and taught nursing for two years after which she went to the General Hospital in Vancouver where she took a post graduate course in Obstetrics.

Laura returned to Calgary in early 1933 and for five years was Obstetrical Supervisor at the Holy Cross Hospital.

In the fall of 1938 she went to Toronto to attend the University of Toronto where she got her Public Health Nursing Degree.

Further studies were undertaken in 1949, when on an Alberta Government fellowship she went to the New York Maternity Centre, New York and the Kentucky Frontier Centre, Hyden, Kentucky to study their program in midwifery.

Had Laura been a missionary it would have been said that she received a calling to serve in the North and had accepted the call. She arrived at her cottage at the outpost community called Valleyview, 320 miles from Edmonton on September 19, 1939. This was to be her home until she moved to Whitecourt in 1941.

After seven years she left Whitecourt for Smith in 1948 and moved from Smith to Slave Lake in 1950.

Ten years later she left Slave Lake for Wabasca. In 1962 she transferred to Swan Hills for a short stint then back to Slave Lake until 1964. From there she transferred to Paddle Prairie for a few months then on to her last post at High Level, 500 miles north of Edmonton.

From the first posting at Valleyview in 1939 to the last, there is a span of thirty years of frontier nursing. Probably few people in Northern Alberta have seen more suffering than this outstanding nurse. Probably no nurse has accepted the challenge to eliminate suffering and disease in Northern Alberta so diligently and perhaps with so much enjoyment as has Laura Attrux.

Laura has served as nurse, acted as a student counsellor, as a marriage counsellor, as a veterinarian, as a dentist, as a surgeon, as a physician, as a midwife, as a community leader and mostly has been a friend.

True Laura might meet a patient at the door at 4:00 o'clock in

Nurse Laura Margaret Attrux in May, 1970 when she received an Honorary Doctors degree from the University of Alberta.

the morning and grumble about it. Many of us have been scolded by her for this but never has a patient been turned away from her door and maybe Laura hadn't had a decent night's sleep in a week but the patients wouldn't be told that.

It has been brought to our attention that at Whitecourt her largest patient was a horse with a deep muscle cut and her smallest was a canary with a broken leg — she splinted it with a toothpick.

This devoted nurse as a Centennial project adopted a child in South America; took flying lessons several years ago and bought a Cessna 150; and is a successful business woman. She remains an adventurer.

It is interesting to note that Laura has been awarded the Coronation medal by the Queen for service to humanity and she has also been given the Pope John 23rd medal for twenty years service to the health of persons in remote areas.

In 1970 at a Convocation at the University of Alberta, Laura Attrux was given an Honorary Doctor of Laws degree for over thirty years' service in the Medical field in remote spots in Northern Alberta.

The whole community is very proud of Dr. Laura Margaret Attrux, and are happy that she is enjoying retirement at High Level.

A DIFFERENT BREED OF PEOPLE

Recently, only in December of 1975, Mr. Justice Emmett Hall was completing hearings on rail line transportation and grain handling at Fairview.

Two farmers from the High Level - Fort Vermilion area travelled more than 300 miles to tell the Hall Commission that they would like to have a better road between Fort Vermilion and High Level so that they can haul their grain in larger trucks.

Ted Bond and Aubrey Milner said "We're not complaining, we're not asking for a railroad, all we want is a road heavy enough to stand grain and forest product traffic."

Mr. Bond told the commission how he left his farm forty-five miles east of High Level at 6:30 in the morning to get to the elevator to dump a load of rapeseed. When he got there his truck was forty-eighth in line waiting to unload. He raced back to pick up another load of rapeseed and when he got back to the elevator at 1:00 A.M. the following day he was already eighth in line.

In summary, Mr. Hall made a good comment to Mr. Bond and Mr. Milner covering all the farmers in the area. "I think you are a different breed of people down there." He suggested that in other areas of the Prairies farmers are upset if they have to haul a half dozen miles.

This is a nice tribute to all our farmers we think.

ALMOST McCLARTYVILLE

Probably one of Alberta's longest distance - most challenging commuters in recent times was Albert McClarty.

Albert and family lived in the Manning area since 1934, and in 1958 could see an extra spark of movement in the North in the vicinity of a wide spot in the Mackenzie Highway at the junction of the North-South road and the turn-off to Rocky Lane and Fort Vermilion. This wide spot was High Level.

Albert took over the Imperial Oil Bulk Station and distributed fuels far and wide to the scattered oil rigs, seismic outfits, farms, outpost settlements and to the few residents of the town. Air craft would land on Thompson Field across the highway and taxi across to the bulk station for aviation fuel.

In 1959 when his family was nearly through school he and his wife, Evelyn, took up permanent residence in High Level and Evelyn was appointed Postmistress in a little partitioned off cubicle of her living room on the Imperial Oil bulk yard.

Shortly after, Albert's eldest son Ernie, and wife Hazel, moved from Manning to High Level and Ernie bought the Imperial Service Station and Hazel accepted the position of teacher in the one room school.

Cecil, the next eldest son, quit his job with the Government in Edmonton and began negotiations in early 1964 to build the first

Beattie Cumming, left, first secretary of the New Town of High Level and Albert McClarty, first Chairman of the Board, New Town of High Level in 1966.

High Level Post Office on Main Street. September, 1966.

all-hardware store in far Northern Alberta. He opened this store in late 1964.

Albert's eldest daughter, Arlene, was married and lived in the East but their second daughter, Carol, completed her grade eleven in Manning and came to work in the little general store next to the Esso garage.

As the town developed in 1963 it became apparent that someone must be appointed to represent the government in development control and the likely candidate was Albert. He was appointed Development Control Officer in June, 1963, a post he held until 1965 when the Town was declared "The New Town of High Level," and at its helm was Albert McClarty as Chairman of the Board of Administrators.

The third son, Barry, joined his father in 1964 in the oil business and Barry took on a wife, Lorna, whom he had met in Edmonton. She too became a teacher in the newly expanded school.

Robert, the fourth son, entered University and returned at the end of the term to practice teach.

Judy assisted her mother in the post office.

During the course of a few years this family was active in nearly all phases of the community, the Chamber of Commerce, the United Church, the Fire Department, the Curling rink, the community hall, the Centennial Committee, the Elk's Lodge, the skating rink and the ball tournaments.

It is little wonder that as a Halloween prank during the height of the McClarty project in the growth of this new community, that

Former Mathison Pool Room purchased by Franke's and moved to main street in 1964. Here Ethel Franke is readying concrete.

someone took down the "High Level" sign post at the south entrance to the town, and in its place put a sign "McClartyville."

No other family has had such complete involvement in a community as has this fine family.

THE WIVES OF PIONEERS

Back in 1966, Owen Jordan took a few minutes to meditate on the pioneering experiences of he and his wife Fanny. After completing the harsh homestead duties they embarked upon the operation of a general store, motel, and service station business with cafe which took long hours under crude conditions. Of course there was no sewer and water, no pavement, no television, little radio, and no medical facilities. When they sold this operation they embarked upon the grand venture of a $400,000 hotel and complex at the wide spot on the Mackenzie Highway.

One bit of the conversation stands out most emphatically. Said Owen of this country, "there's going to be work for lots of men but they'll have to be the type of men who aren't discouraged by isolation . . . and lack of television. Also it's no place for a married man, unless he's got the right kind of wife. If she isn't suited to this primitive country, the man is beaten before he starts."

Taken from Maclean's Magazine, Feb. 16/66.

THE UNDERWEAR THAT BUILT A ROAD

Rumors circulated in early 1965 that with the Rainbow Lake Oil Boom a road from the oil field should be built either southeast to Keg River, or east to the Mackenzie Highway at High Level.

It was urgent to High Level that the connection be made here, and furthermore, it was urgent that those at the Indian settlements of Habay and Assumption be consulted in the road plan and hopefully be induced to see that High Level was their future centre.

Mrs. Valle Gray was a good friend of some of the band councillors, and it therefore became her duty to accompany Gordon Reid to a meeting set by Chief Harry Chonkolay with the Bands at the garage at Assumption.

This meeting was set for February 15th and upon awakening that morning the thermometer sat at 59 degrees below zero F.

Surely it was foolish to start out in this weather for a meeting and it was suggested that the trip be called off. School was cancelled and that should have been some indication.

A curt reply was received from Mrs. Gray, saying simply: "I went downtown yesterday and bought a suit of this new-fangled underwear from Roy Harbourne at Roy's Men's Wear and I have no intention of backing out on that trip. It is important to High Level. Let's get going!"

Away we went taking twelve year old Donald Reid with us. We

Mrs. Valle Gray in her new "underwear" with Donald Reid crossing the Chinchaga River at 59 degrees Below F.

took hot coffee and emergency supplies, and arrived at the meeting approximately ten minutes before it was to start.

All councillors showed up as well as about fifty others. The meeting was chaired by Chief Chonkolay. Our case was explained and after about four hours a vote by the councillors was in favour of the east-west route.

Had this plucky old doll backed out of that trip an important link in our communication may not have been a reality.

SINNERS

An old friend of the Quists received a letter from Premier Peter Lougheed which began "Dear Senior Citizen," A new program is . . . ."

The friend could not read very well but took exception to the insinuation in the letter title.

The old gent came to his neighbours quite upset with Mr. Lougheed.

"I just don't mind the government meddlin' in most of my affairs but I think it's goin' too fur when he starts writing letters saying:

"Dear Sinner Citizens."

INGA

The North misses a character who lived with us since 1958 and operated a Trading Post at Indian Cabins. Inga Lund retired to Peace River at seventy years of age after operating her post for fourteen years.

Just about everybody knew Inga Lund.

Despite being the sole white resident of Alberta's most northerly trading post she claims that loneliness was never a problem at Indian Cabins.

"I had lots and lots of friends," she laughs; in an accent that betrays her Norwegian origin.

The bus drivers were "all my boys" and each day one dropped into her small store at Mile 288 on the Mackenzie Highway to bring her news from up and down the line.

Add this to the hundreds of oilmen, commercial travellers, tourists and road workers who came to know her during her stay at Indian Cabins and it's easy to see why she always kept the coffee pot on.

"That old road was terrible when I first came here. The bus drivers had to stay over two or three days when culverts washed out."

"In all my years at Indian Cabins I never had to call the police. When the police did come it was only for a visit." "I was the only policeman to keep an eye on the Indians," she chuckled to herself.

Inga Lund, Indian Cabins Trader, 1958 to 1972.

"While I was at Indian Cabins I delivered three babies. These were things you just had to do. My only neighbours were a small group of Slaveys living nearby."

Her trading post was just nine miles from the Northwest Territories Border and her yard was originally a Hudson's Bay Post for the region.

"Yes," she meditates "I was policeman, returning officer, postmaster, cook, grocer, ticket agent, nurse, companion." "It was hard work," she said "but it was kind of a stopping place — always something I could do for someone."

Truly this was a great old gal of the North - she enjoyed her isolation but also she enjoyed her friends.

POPULATION EXPLOSION

The population of High Level has grown over the years. With

High Level, Summer of 1964. Looking S.W. Hotel in right foreground. Grader working on Main Street just completed.

sixty people in 1962, seventy-five in 1963 the oil boom arrived in 1965 with Banff Oil discovery at Rainbow Lake and continued for four years.

The population of the town jumped from 754 in 1966 to 1,551 in 1967.

FUNERAL WITH FRIENDS

Times were tough just a few years ago - in 1969 especially. The oil boom had gone from High Level, but worse than that the farmers who were struggling against the weather at the best of times had experienced their fifth straight crop failure. It had broken the spirit of many and maybe one of the ones who had worked the hardest but just couldn't get a crop was a dear friend of High Level - John Gibb.

During the night of July 3rd, 1969 John rested on a couch in the living room and his wife, Gladys, heard him groan as she read in bed. She got up quickly and found him severely distressed. There were no 'phones on the farms then and she had son, Bruce, drive into town for Nurse Laura.

Laura arrived too late and pronounced John dead.

Laura made him comfortable after dressing him neatly. She folded his hands peacefully and said a prayer.

The family was heartbroken at the loss, and were in very bad shape financially also. A decision was made in a true pioneer fashion by Gladys. There would be a simple low-cost funeral at old Fort Vermilion where John's father had been buried.

A plain coffin was ordered in Peace River and it came to High Level on Tony's Trucking. Friends came to the farm to place John's heavy body into the coffin and many came to the house to pay their respects and to say farewell to a good neighbour.

The day of the funeral many people gathered on the lawn when the casket was taken from the living room out through the little-used front door, and put into the back of Reid's station wagon.

Two good friends of John, Alex Orlesky and Gordon Reid drove John to the Fort. The two had a good trip that day - they talked of crops and crop failures; the possibilities of T.V.; of pavement; of growth of the North; of the arrival of the railroad - all the things so dear to their friend in the back.

Present at the funeral were John and Gladys' Mennonite friends from Buffalo Prairie, and LaCrete, friends from Rocky Lane and Fort Vermilion; their Indian friends from various reserves; and as well their newer friends from High Level and district.

John was a plain man and would appreciate this simple funeral with all of his friends around.

SENIOR PRAYER

Grandma Reid has this verse handy as she has her seventy-fifth birthday, and is still in good health.

> Lord, Thou knowest I am growing old,
> Keep me from becoming talkative
> And possessed with the idea, that
> I must express myself on every subject.
> Release me from the craving to
> Straighten out everyone's affairs
> Keep me from the recital of endless detail
> Give me wings to get to the point.
> Seal my lips when I am inclined
> To tell of my aches and pains,
> They are increasing with the years
> And the love to speak of them
> Grows sweeter as the time goes by.
> Teach me the glorious lesson
> That occasionally I may be wrong,
> Make me thoughtful, thoughtful but
> Not nosey, helpful: but not bossy.
> With my vast store of wisdom and experience
> It does seem a pity not to use it all,
> But Thou knowest, Lord, that I want
> A few friends at the end.

BLACK MARKET TELEPHONES

Because of the frantic oil boom which started in January 1965, telephones became a "Black Market" item in High Level up until Alberta Government Telephones could get new lines installed in early 1967.

Private telephone numbers were being sold for $100.00 each for use by companies in or related to the oil industry.

During 1965 and 1966 the best time to make a 'phone call was between midnight and 7:30 A.M., for any other time lines were jambed with calls.

In the daytime it took an hour at least most of the time to get the operator.

Of course there were over one hundred oil company related businesses operating out of High Level, and it is easy to understand the frantic necessity of having a telephone.

A BEAUTIFUL COMMUNION

As is common in all new communities, the church's attempt to become established and the traits of the older churches are brought with the new residents. The followers of the United Church met in 1963 once a month in the one-roomed school or in the homes of those interested in the fellowship of the Church. At

Simple R.C. Church, High Level Catholic Service 10:00 A.M. Protestant (Assorted) Service 11:15 A.M.

first, the minister came from Manning or Peace River, also members would take the service.

During early 1965 the United Church received an invitation from the Roman Catholic Church to use their Church to hold Sunday services. The offer was accepted and a student minister arrived for summer services.

Come fall, the student was about to leave and an invitation to preach was extended to Rev. John Cohen who had been sent to High Level by the Anglican Church.

To celebrate the event of having an Anglican Minister, preach a United service, in the Catholic Church, it was agreed that there should be a service of Communion.

All plans went well until it was realized that there were no communion vessels nearer than Fort Vermilion or Manning. Not to be discouraged in a community that improvised, a souvenir plate was purchased from the hardware store to serve as the Communion tray. We tried to devise some means of serving the grape juice and at last the answer was found - Ernie Duchesne had discovered a tube of fifty unused, half-ounce wolf poison pellet cups which were left over from a former rabies outbreak.

These were filled with grape juice and a beautiful service was held.

The plate was given to a dear little lady, Mrs. Gill, who was leaving for her home after spending the summer in High Level, and she prized it greatly as a reminder of a historic movement in a new frontier.

First building in High Level 1950. Jimmy Jones and Don Staples Cafe.

THE LONG TIMER

Longest time resident of High Level is Don Staples who farms east of High Level along the Fort Vermilion road.

Don, along with Jimmy Jones and Jimmy's wife, Florence,

Jimmy Jones who along with Don Staples established the cafe and cabins at High Level in 1950. Taken at Steen River in 1967.

Cabin of High Level Motel just completed in the fall of 1950.

came to High Level in July of 1950 and lived in a tent while they were building the cafe. When that building was completed they moved to rooms above the cafe. In 1951 they built the cabins which were to become the simple High Level Motel.

When they arrived in High Level there was only one shack-like structure which was owned by Trader George Clarke for storing supplies on trips from Fort Vermilion to Hay Lakes.

Don sold his share of the business to Jimmy in 1953 and then Jimmy sold out to Steve Keleman in 1954. Jimmy moved to Meander River for a time where he purchased the pool room/store from Sam Fedorus, then on to Steen River.

Sitting in Don's yard on the farm east of High Level is a small cabin which was purchased from Blakney's who had a stopping place seventeen miles down north on the Mackenzie Highway. It was bought by Keleman and used as living quarters for crew at High Level for a few years.

Keleman's Staff Quarters, 1954.

THE MAGNETIC FRONTIER

"There is some drawing force in this area; almost like a magnet." So said Mrs. Vic Jumago in 1964. It was easy then to add "Frontier" for surely we were and are in the great frontier area of Canada.

LEGION LADIES

If there is ever a group of women to be honoured in High Level it would have to be the ladies of the auxiliary of the Royal Canadian Legion.

Such constant devotion to just plain hard work is seldom found today.

THE OPEN-AIR PAVILION

Lots of hard work went into the sports ground two miles north of High Level, and one of the features of the grounds was an elevated pavilion used as a dance floor for open-air dances up until the fall of 1963.

Dances went on nearly all night for everyone found that the later the night, the fewer the mosquitoes.

You had to pay to get inside a pole rail fence surrounding the pavilion, and if you decided to stay outside the rail fence you could hardly hear the music.

There were no amplifiers for there wasn't any power.

Bingos were held there too.

A United Church Picnic at the open air pavilion Sports Ground, north of High Level 1964.

SHORTY MacDONALD

Always a pleasure to meet on the street is long time High Level resident, T.A. (Shorty) MacDonald. In fact, Shorty was here before there were streets, having arrived here in 1962.

THE RESCUE

Ernie Lanti, now a farmer at High Level, began cat-skinning in 1951 when he was only seventeen.

He told of an incident in 1954, north of what is now Zama, when one T.D. 18 cat became bogged down in a muskeg. It was nearly buried.

Another T.D. 18 cat attempted to come to its rescue and it, too, sank.

A third T.D. 18 left solid ground to attempt rescue, and it fell through and was nearly submerged.

T.D. 18 Cat mired in muskeg north of Zama, 1954. Ernie Lanti far right.

Mike Henitiuk was foreman for owner, Ted Eigeard, and it was realized the situation was desperate.

They had moved into the area through Meander River to do seismic clearing and a call was put out for rescue cats. The rescue cats arrived through a trail from Steen River.

It would have been pointless to send another cat onto the muskeg, and it was decided to build a corduroy road so that when a cat was freed of the muskeg it could be walked to higher ground.

The muskeg was immense, and for over three miles trees stripped of branches had to be skidded and put into place to form a corduroy road.

The crew of fourteen worked constantly for ten days and were exhausted when the three heavy machines were again in operation.

Ernie says that wages were $1.35 per hour, and that was good money, and the cats were earning $11.00 per hour.

By today's standard this rescue would have cost $65,000 in extra wages, lost time and machine repairs.

LEAVE SOMETHING BEHIND

In a simple review of High Level by newcomer, Pastor Gerry Mitchinson, in August of 1975, he says: "It is said that the average length of stay for a northern resident is two or three years. There's hope that this will change. But if it doesn't, it means that we haven't much time to leave behind something of ourselves."

Hank Thompson Hanger 1964.

THAT'S IT FOR NOW

Only the surface has been scratched with this bit of information of the Magnetic Frontier.

No stories have been included of Andrew Sarapuk, the pilot Papirny, the trappers, the fires, Ukrainian Christmas, the Lizottes, family reunions, the Polish Santa Claus, Hank Thompson, Roy Harbourne, the Mathesons, the Shannons, the Quists, the Bouchers, the Maguires and on and on . . . but there's no more room, so that's it for now.